31143009288334
378.1616 Ravikumar
Ravikumar, Nived, author.
50 questions for your
admissions essay draft

D0224485

50 QUESTIONS FOR YOUR ADMISSIONS ESSAY DRAFT

Nived Ravikumar

50 Questions for Your Admissions Essay Draft: The Most Practical Checklist for College and Graduate School Admissions Essays

Published by ProTagYou Press

Distributed by Statement Guru

Copyright © 2014 Nived Ravikumar

ALL RIGHTS RESERVED

No part of this publication may be reproduced, stored in a retrieval system or transmitted, in any form or by any means— electronic, mechanical, photocopying, recording or otherwise— without prior written permission, except for the inclusion of brief quotations in a review.

ISBN: 978-0-9906075-1-9

Printed in the United States of America

Cover photo by Michael Modecki

Cover design by Nived Ravikumar & Ariel A. Oye

ABOUT NIVED

As Founder/Guru-In-Chief of StatementGuru.com, Nived Ravikumar has helped dozens of applicants all over the world craft exceptional essays for their college and graduate school applications. He is also a contest-winning comedy screenwriter and Mensa member.

CONTENTS

So you've completed a draft of your admissions essay. Congratulations! Pat yourself on the back. Okay, stop patting, you've still got work to do. Yep... another draft. Or two. Or ten. I know it seems daunting. I've been there myself. So, in writing this book, I tried to imagine the guide I wished I'd had during through those long nights of fear and uncertainty.

Before we get started, a disclaimer—I've worked with many applicants from all over the world through my company Statement Guru, and my methods work. However, there are millions of people applying to all sorts of programs every year. I simply cannot write something that addresses every scenario/prompt/word limit that every applicant out there could possibly encounter. If the essay prompt wants specific information about your research work, future goals, etc., don't neglect it because I happened not to talk about it. Be smart, be flexible, and this book will serve you well.

Okay, ready? Ask the following fifty questions about your admissions essay draft. The more yeses the better. Keep track of the nos, not just in your head, but on a separate piece of paper (like this one: statementguru.com/50-questions-checklist). If you get a lot of yeses, I'm happy for you, but those aren't going to get your essay to the next level. Transforming your nos into yeses will.

If you haven't written a draft yet, even better! Reading this will help you sidestep numerous pitfalls so when you <u>do</u> go through this to evaluate your draft, your task will be that much easier, and the end-result that much better.

IS YOUR ESSAY IN ENGLISH?

O YES O NO

If you are applying to universities in the English-speaking world, your admissions essay <u>must</u> be in English. No exceptions. Okay, that was an easy one, but it's good to start off with a win.

Question Two

DID YOU AVOID PLAGIARIZING YOUR ESSAY?

O YES   O NO

Another easy one. Unless there are plagiarists out there who would actually bother with a book like this. If so, your paradoxical nature fascinates me.

DO YOU LIKE IT? I MEAN, LIKE LIKE IT?

O YES   O NO

For most people, writing an admissions essay is a chore. You get it over with, and the document you're left with is the document you're left with. Could be good, could be bad, the important thing is it's finished. I say, "No way! You should be a huge fan of that thing!" "But Nived, that's impossible! People aren't <u>supposed</u> to like their admissions essays." Then why do my clients say things like, "I love my essay" or "I can't stop reading my essay"? About the process itself, they often use words like "fun," "therapeutic" and "cathartic." Sure, it's a challenge, but it's the kind of challenge that's rewarding if done right.

DOES IT AVOID BEING BORING?

O YES O NO

For the love of God, don't bore people! Attention spans are getting shorter. Many people now legitimately have a hard time reading anything over 140 characters. The last thing you want to do is put your readers to sleep with monotonous technical details and verbose ramblings. There must be a point! It must be engaging! It must not be boring!

DOES IT AVOID BEING A PROSE RESUME?

O YES   O NO

"Prose resume" is a pejorative term I coined for essays that read like resumes. Y'know, dry and mechanical summaries of what you've done. The only real difference between resumes and prose resumes is that instead of bullet points, prose resumes use paragraphs. While a very good writer can make their prose resume entertaining, steer clear no matter what. Not only does a prose resume have a severely limited upside, it misses the point of the exercise entirely. Admissions essays are meant to showcase intangibles like leadership qualities, courage, passion, drive, integrity, empathy and hope. There's a time and a place for facts and figures. It's called the REST OF YOUR APPLICATION.

Question Six

IS IT ABOUT YOU? REALLY?

O YES   O NO

This sounds obvious, but certain prompts can mislead. If the prompt asks about your mentor, in reality, they don't really care about your mentor. They care about how your mentor made <u>you</u> who <u>you</u> are. If they ask you about a challenging work situation, they don't want to hear you complain about your jerk boss. They want to hear about how <u>you</u> dealt with him, what lesson <u>you</u> learned, in short, YOU YOU YOU!

DID YOU RESIST STARTING WITH A QUOTE?

O YES O NO

I'm not against quotes altogether in essays. In fact, some of the essays I've worked on ended with a quote or prominently featured one somewhere in the middle. But I don't believe in starting with one. Sure, Gandhi, Mark Twain, Nelson Mandela and MLK all said some great things, but guess what? They're not applying to college, you are.

It's kind of a shame though, Mark Twain would have written one hell of an admissions essay.

Question Eight

IS YOUR FIRST PARAGRAPH THE MOST IMPORTANT?

O YES O NO

The essay is the face of your application, the thing that gives it personality. The first paragraph of the essay is the face of the face. So it bears the responsibility of being the personality of the personality. I've said this a thousand times, and I'll say it a thousand more: "If you don't grab your reader in the first paragraph, chances are, you never will."

Have you ever watched a movie and were totally not into it? You just didn't care. If the hero was unexpectedly gunned down, you would have been thrilled to leave earlier than expected. But no, heroes are way too resilient for that, leaving you to check your watch every other minute, bored out of your skull. I'm willing to bet that in such cases, your apathy was due to a storytelling failure in the first part of the movie. Well, the same logic applies to essays. Get the first paragraph right.

DOES IT HAVE A THESIS STATEMENT?

O YES O NO

People hear that they need a thesis statement, and they tense up, a look of fear in their eyes. It's similar to the look they'd give if they had just found out they had been diagnosed with a disease. Ironically, it's <u>not</u> having a thesis statement that will kill you. But it's not that hard to think of one, it's just one measly sentence after all. Here's how you know you have a good one:

- It requires support. If it's about how your interest in architecture started with Legos, that's a workable thesis because I'm curious to learn more. Did you compete in Lego design competitions? Do you still play with Legos?

Did Duplo have a role as well? Now compare this to a statement of fact, like, "I owned 550 Lego pieces." Uhh, okay...? There's nowhere to go from here because you didn't take a stand, even a minor one. Remember, your thesis statement starts the argument and the rest of your essay backs it up.

- It illustrates something about you. In history class, you can have a thesis about how World War I was caused by alliances. For our purposes, however, the thesis statement should allow us to understand <u>you</u> on a deeper level. Maybe it could be about how you always wanted to be a superhero. Or about how being an immigrant made you an outsider growing up. Or about how you _____.

I gave you a running start there, hope you filled it with something good!

DOES YOUR THESIS STATEMENT PASS THE ELEVATOR TEST?

O YES O NO

A helpful way of framing your thesis statement is with something I call the Elevator Test. You're visiting your dream school, frolicking through the department building when—the Dean enters the elevator you're riding! It's just you and her. Now this is an unusually powerful Dean. She can snap his fingers, and you're in with a full-ride scholarship. She turns to you, "Applying here, huh? Tell me, what's your admissions essay about?" You only have 15 seconds or so until the elevator reaches the ground floor, and she'll be your audience no more. What do you say? Is it finger-snap-worthy?

Question Eleven
IS YOUR THESIS STATEMENT UNIQUE TO YOU?

O YES O NO

Usually, the thesis statements I decipher from the essays I evaluate are some variation of, "I really like computer programming [or whatever subject], and I want to learn more about it." Imagine you're an admissions officer, and you have to read hundreds of essays. How many of those essays' thesis statements can be summarized in this exact same manner? If the thesis statement is the face of the essay and it's generic, how is the rest of the essay going to read?

Question Twelve

IS YOUR THESIS STATEMENT IN THE FIRST PARAGRAPH?

O YES O NO

It's possible to have your thesis statement anywhere in your essay. It's even possible to have an implied thesis statement, where you don't actually state it, but readers get it. But most people will be best served placing the thesis statement at the very end of their first paragraph. Think about movie trailers. Your first paragraph should be your essay's movie trailer. Explosions! Big stars! Romance! Want more? Go see the movie/read the rest of the essay!

IS THE FIRST PARAGRAPH EVOCATIVE?

O YES O NO

Okay, maybe that last analogy confused you a bit. "I need to find big stars for my first paragraph?" No, though it can't hurt. But your opener should include metaphorical explosions and romance. It can be as simple as an insight or discovery you had, or a memory, even a dream for the future. Remember to engage the senses, deal in emotions, court controversy. Don't go overboard with this though, you want it to come across as interesting and real, not calculated and manufactured. Bold, not bombastic.

DOES THE FIRST PARAGRAPH WORK IN CONJUNCTION WITH YOUR THESIS STATEMENT?

O YES O NO

Assuming your thesis statement is contained in your first paragraph, you should treat the statement itself as the queen and the rest of the paragraph's sentences as the bishops, knights, rooks and pawns. Before busting out that powerful queen, have her minions do the groundwork. And who's the king? You are, once you get that prized acceptance letter! I realize this analogy is a bit gender-biased, but in all fairness, I did make the all-powerful Dean earlier a woman.

DOES THE SECOND PARAGRAPH REORIENT THE READER?

O YES O NO

A by-product of a bold first paragraph is that it can sometimes leave the reader disoriented. What's going on here? What's this person talking about? Why is this paragraph so evocative? All of these are good sensations for the reader. Think about the movie trailer example—movie trailers pique your curiosity so you're compelled to discover more. Disorientation can be your friend, as long as your second paragraph reorients the reader. Maybe that's where you start your life story, maybe that's where you talk about your high school years. I'm not going to tell you what exactly to put in your second paragraph, but if your first paragraph grabbed readers, you've bought yourself some flexibility here to be less flashy and more normal in order to ease your readers into the rest of the essay.

DOES IT PASS THE DECAPITATION TEST?

O YES O NO

Go ahead and delete your first paragraph. I'll wait. Okay, you're back. I hope you made a backup because you're going to need that paragraph again. You didn't? Undo, undo! Now, backup your file, THEN delete your first paragraph. Your essay should be noticeably worse because —as we've established—your first paragraph is the most important one. But look at what's left of your essay. Does it make sense? If so, congrats, your essay just passed the Decapitation Test. Right now, you're probably thinking, that was the most pointless test ever. But it's not. It's in fact very important for establishing the relationship between the first and second paragraphs. The first supplies the sizzle, the second the steak. You need both, without overlap. The Decapitation Test is a grim but simple way of checking that.

Question Seventeen

DOES IT AVOID THESAURUS WORDS?

O YES O NO

By all means, use a thesaurus if it helps you find normal words there's a chance you would have thought of using anyway. But be careful with that thesaurus, because within that thing, there are thousands upon thousands of words that no human being would ever normally utter— UNLESS they were trying to impress someone. Guess what? Admissions officers have seen it all, and they can see right through your subterfuge, and they're not impressed.

DOES IT MAINTAIN CONSISTENT PARAGRAPH LENGTHS?

O YES O NO

Inconsistent paragraph lengths are jarring. When someone taps their foot or claps their hands to music, it's steady, right? Well, your paragraphs are beats, too. Big, word-laden beats. And if you can get each one to the same general length, the flow of your essay will dramatically improve. This isn't an exact science, and every paragraph having the exact same word count would be a bit weird. But having them be in the same general neighborhood can be tremendously beneficial for readability. It's very common for me to give new life to an ineffective client essay simply by tweaking paragraphs to get them closer to the magic number. My default magic number is 165 words per paragraph FYI.

I should add that if you're quite comfortable with your writing skills, you can probably disregard this advice. In fact, short paragraphs, used sparingly, can really liven things up.

Question Nineteen

IS IT TRUE?

O YES O NO

Some embellishment is par for the course. But past a certain threshold, it crosses over into dishonesty. You shouldn't need to be out-and-out dishonest, but if you decide to be a bit sneaky, do it in ways that are impossible for anyone to verify. For example, you might have reached a decision in your life that required months of careful thought. In essay form, that entire process might be represented as just one "A-ha!" moment. No one would question that in the first place, but even if they did, who would actually snitch and say, "No, Jane was in fact looking quite ponderous well before that day"? No one. Just remember: dishonesty bad, poetic license good.

Question Twenty
IS IT MEMORABLE?

O YES O NO

In Freshman English, I was assigned to read "A Modest Proposal" by Jonathan Swift. It's probably one of the most famous essays ever. In it, Swift argues that in order to solve Ireland's economic woes, poor children should be eaten as food. This classic example of satire was written in 1729, and people STILL remember it. Don't worry, your essay doesn't need that kind of longevity, but the more it linger in your readers' minds, the better.

Three points:

1. There is also such a thing as memorable in a bad way. Yeah, avoid that.

2. No references to cannibalism. Unless you saved yourself or someone else from being eaten.

3. Distinguishing characteristics are the key to making your essay memorable. If you can frame your essay around that month you spent on the Trans-Siberian Railway, that's certainly memorable. If you can talk about that year you spent becoming fluent in Esperanto, also memorable. Memorable can work in smaller ways as well. In one essay I worked on, the reason my client first became interested in architecture was because she witnessed the construction of one of the world's largest bridges when she was younger. It's not like she had anything to do with building the bridge, but bringing it up still helped define the essay. Similarly, one of my clients was inspired to study graphics because of his love of science fiction films. Even just talking about *The Matrix* and *The Terminator* in an admissions essay can make it memorable because no one else is doing it.

IS YOUR ESSAY ONE PIECE?

O YES O NO

This question considers not just the thesis statement, but tone and flow. When reading your essay, does it feel like a singular experience, or does it feel like a schizophrenic mishmash? Oftentimes, I'll evaluate an essay in which one paragraph is a heart-rendering memory, then the next is a listing of every class they took in excruciating detail, then the next is a recipe for Chicken Marsala. Leave the channel surfing to the couch potatoes, let your readers enjoy uninterrupted, commercial-free programming.

DOES YOUR ESSAY ANSWER ALL PARTS OF THE PROMPT?

O YES O NO

If they want to know your research interests, tell them that. If they want to know your most negative trait, tell them that. If they want to know who your favorite member of One Direction is and why, tell them! (Although I question your decision to apply to whatever program asked you that.) Believe me when I say you can address everything they ask of you <u>and</u> everything I ask of you. And if you really can't, favor them because, if you can't follow basic instructions, you're either dumb or a rebel. They don't have patience for either.

DOES IT PAINT PICTURES?

O YES   O NO

The best kind of writing takes you there, wherever there is. A tropical island for a summer of volunteer work. Your first piano recital. That spring break when you hit the ~~beach~~ books. Your role is not to summarize defining events in your life. Your role is be a storyteller, to pluck the reader out of their world and momentarily allow them to inhabit yours. One of the most effective ways to elevate your writing into storytelling is the use of imagery. Colors, shadows, textures, adjectives, expressions, descriptions, brand names, fashion cues, symbols, light—these are the brushes in your box.

DOES IT MAKE SOUNDS?

O YES O NO

While visuals give the reader sight, we shouldn't neglect the other senses. Touch, taste and smell are bonuses, but after sight, if there's one to get right, it's sound. Some carefully placed audio cues can do wonders. A car shouldn't just stop. It should <u>screech</u> to a halt. Instead of being left in silence, try being left in <u>agonizing</u> silence. A window should never just break, it should <u>shatter</u>. Why would a person yell when they can <u>howl</u>? I hope my point is being made with a <u>deafening thud</u>.

Question Twenty-Five

DOES EACH PARAGRAPH HAVE A DISTINCT FUNCTION?

O YES O NO

Imagine the members of a basketball team. However different their playing styles and backgrounds might be from one another, at the end of the day, all they care about is winning, winning, winning. Now, take your essay. Its mission is also singular: to support a winning thesis statement. Each paragraph works in support of that purpose. But just as each team member's role on a basketball court is different—ball handler, 3-point specialist, rim protector—each paragraph's role in your essay should be different. It is helpful to think of 2-3 words to describe each paragraph. For example: 1. thesis paragraph, 2. high school, 3. undergraduate years, 4. thesis project, 5. work experience/crossroads, 6. future plans. If you have two undergraduate years paragraphs or your undergraduate years paragraph is way longer than any other paragraph, that's a sign that there's some ball-hogging going on.

DOES IT AVOID REVEALING TMI (TOO MUCH INFORMATION)?

O YES O NO

Beware the confessional essay. In this type, the writer sits down, then proceeds to pour their heart out. Maybe they come out of the closet, maybe they confess to a crime, maybe they admit they secretly don't want to go to school anymore. Whatever the case, this is extremely dangerous territory. It's good to be candid, honest and authentic, but doing so to this extent actually has the opposite effect: it indicates you're not authentic to everyone else in your life. Colleges don't want to have a sleepover with you so you can tell each other your deepest, darkest secrets. They want you to be mature enough to have taken steps to resolve that stuff already. And if you <u>have</u> overcome such life challenges and it has made you congruent in the way you now live your life, heck, it probably <u>is</u> a viable essay topic.

DOES IT DEMONSTRATE YOU OVERCOMING ADVERSITY?

O YES O NO

In the movies, a hero is only as heroic as the villain is villainous. If James Bond didn't have a steady stream of baddies to foil, he'd just sip martinis and seduce women repetitively. He'd be Hugh Hefner basically. Batman needs his Joker, Spiderman his Green Goblin, Superman his Lex Luthor. So ask yourself, who or what is your evil counterpart? It doesn't have to be super dramatic, like a deadly disease. It can be anything from a difficult class to a rival to stage fright to writer's block. The easiest villain to feature in your essay is complacency. If you're motivated, complacency is your enemy. In the absence of

anything else, that's fine, but since it's also kind of easy,
you only get half-credit.

IN YOUR ESSAY, DO YOU TRY HARD WITHOUT BEING A TRY-HARD?

O YES O NO

What?

Let me explain—Trying hard is good. It shows passion and dedication, and if you combine those things with intelligence, that's the admissions trifecta right there. But let's not mistake trying hard with being a try-hard. You know that annoying guy who constantly mentions how much he can bench press? Try-hard. That pretentious co-worker who gushes about her recent trip to the French Riviera? Try-hard. Now, there's nothing wrong with fancy trips, fast cars, big houses and feats of strength per se, but when the sole purpose of mentioning those things is to impress others, it reeks of insecurity, desperation and neediness. So, go for the trifecta, steer clear of the try-hard-fecta.

Question Twenty-Nine

DOES IT AVOID UNDERSELLING YOU?

O YES O NO

This is the counter-example to the try-hard question. While you don't want to brag, you also don't want to be too modest. Strike a balance where you talk about your accomplishments, but do so in a way that gives credit to your collaborators, ruminates on lessons learned from that experience, expresses self-fulfillment without being self-aggrandizing. Look at it like this: <u>the spotlight is on you, but you're not the only one onstage</u>. I know that overselling vs. underselling is a tricky balance to reach. When in doubt, err on the side of overselling though. This is a competitive admissions process, after all, not a modesty contest.

DOES IT PASS THE EYE TEST?

O YES O NO

Print out your essay or zoom out in Word/Google Docs. Visualize the blocks of text as shapes. Visualize the space between them as, well, space. Is there a sense of symmetry and order in the composition? If not, in your rewrite, figure out a more aesthetically pleasing interplay between the text and the space between. Yes, I've already addressed the importance of similarly-sized paragraphs. This is another way of looking at it (literally). It doesn't really make logical sense, but trust me here—essays that read good look good, too.

DOES IT STAY POSITIVE IN THE PRESENT?

O YES   O NO

Maintaining positivity can sometimes be tricky because many of you are writing about some serious adversity you've battled through. Yes, a lot of the time, bitterness is a natural response to many of life's challenges, and you want to stay true to that in some way. HOWEVER, you must leave the bitterness in the past and present your experiences from a positive, enlightened perspective. The famous Nietzsche quote applies here. "That which does not kill us makes us stronger." You are speaking from a position of strength, positivity and confidence. Also notice, I included a quote, but I didn't start the book with one!

Question Thirty-Two

IS EVERYTHING SPELLED RIGHT? IS THE GRAMMAR IMMACULATE?

O YES O NO

This is hugely important, but I don't have a whole lot to say about it other than DO IT!

Question Thirty-Three

DOES IT SUPPLY THE WHY AND THE HOW?

O YES O NO

Recently, I evaluated an essay in which the applicant says something like, "After being undecided about my major for a while, I finally opted for Criminal Justice." My first reaction was WHY? And I'm sure I'm not alone. Of all the hundreds of degrees to chose from, there must be something propelling her towards that one in particular. Does she have relatives in law enforcement? Was she thinking about law school down the line? She doesn't supply any sort of explanation about what is perhaps the biggest decision of her entire life. Later, she talks about working at a juvenile detention facility and how she bonded with a problem kid and now he has turned his life around. Guess what I thought... yeah, HOW? I see these tendencies all the time, the WHO, WHAT and WHERE are the easy ones. They exist in the physical world. They deal in concrete details. It's the WHY and the HOW that represent a bigger challenge to many applicants because they require greater depth. But that's where the goodness is found.

Question Thirty-Four

IS THE LANGUAGE CONSISTENT WITH ITSELF?

O YES O NO

I work with many clients from India. There are some quirks I encounter in Indian English. For example, it's common to say "under-graduation" instead of "undergrad." Some Indians say "the society" instead of "society." Oh, and a love of right-justified paragraphs is universal throughout the Sub-Continent. I find these quirks endearing and have no interest in "fixing" them. And I think that's for the best because admissions essays are more about personality than perfect English. BUT you must remain consistent. If it's "the society" once, then that's how it's gotta stay. If you dance with the Oxford Comma early on, you're stuck with that Oxford

Comma the entire night. One space or two after a period? I prefer one, but if you go two, that's fine, just stay faithful to that second space!

DOES IT HAVE A PHANTOM TITLE?

O YES O NO

Before you send it off, you can decide whether or not to include a title, if you have one. Generally, your finished version doesn't need one, but if you have a killer title, it can be hard to resist jettisoning it. But before all that, consider having a "phantom title" throughout the rest of the writing process, a shorthand way of keeping track of your thesis statement. It can be a bad pun, a line from a song you like, a snippet from a famous quote. It can be as ho-hum as "taking the stage." That was the phantom title for an essay I recently worked on. In it, my client's dream of becoming a professor was made less daunting by the confidence she gained from competing in music competitions. See how "taking the stage" relates to both performing live and standing before a class to deliver a lecture? With three short words, so much is conveyed about the essay's purpose. So simple, yet so effective as a signpost to keep things on track.

DOES IT DEMONSTRATE YOUR CAPACITY TO "GIVE BACK"?

O YES O NO

Giving back can mean different things in different contexts. In your admissions essay, try to include your version of it. Did you volunteer at a homeless shelter? Did you help your little cousin with her homework? Did you devote time to a club during college? If you've been much too busy to even contemplate activities outside of work/school, don't worry, you can alternatively suggest a plan to give back in the future. The larger point here is that it's good to demonstrate in some way that you care about people. If you really don't care about people, you can surely at least spin your career goals to make it sound like people will directly benefit from what you'll do. You can conveniently leave out the part about how you only really care about their money. I'm looking at you, MBA applicants! Just kidding, you guys are alright.

DOES EVERY PARAGRAPH ACKNOWLEDGE THE THESIS STATEMENT IN SOME WAY?

O YES   O NO

I call this weaving. After you establish your thesis statement in your first paragraph, you need to expand the scope of your essay in subsequent paragraphs. But, like a catchy chorus, the reader shouldn't carry on for too long without a hint of what this essay is really about.

DOES THE ENDING REFERENCE THE BEGINNING?

O YES   O NO

If the very end of your essay can reference the opening in some clever way, you'll finish on such a high note that admissions officers might stand up and cheer. For some reason, in creative works, people love it when things brought up earlier get referenced again. Narratives do this all the time. In the words of Anton Chekhov, "If you say in the first chapter that there is a rifle hanging on the wall, in the second or third chapter it absolutely must go off." Stand-up comics practice the art of the callback all the time. "Oh wow, it's that thing he mentioned 10 minutes ago! He was talking about something totally

different and then it magically came up again! Genius!"
No, not genius, just good planning. And if you plan well,
you can do a callback as good as any comic. One thing to
keep in mind here, when I say you should reference the
opening, that doesn't necessarily have to mean the thesis
statement specifically, though it can.

DOES IT DIFFERENTIATE ITSELF?

O YES   O NO

Does it offer things that the rest of your application doesn't? If you have to submit more than one essay, does this one contain unique content that illuminates a distinct aspect of yourself? If not, that means this essay is redundant, which means you're not taking full advantage of the opportunity. And if you've written a prose resume, I take great joy in now depriving you of a second 'yes' for your sin.

DO YOU TRANSFORM IN IT?

O YES O NO

Transformation is the cornerstone of good storytelling. You take a character. Throw a bunch of obstacles at that character. That character is forced to grow. That growth leads to victory over the obstacles. Are there counter-examples to this transformation thing? Sure... *Being There*, *Dumb and Dumber*, *A Clockwork Orange*, *Psycho*. So... unless you're a complete moron or a psychopath, consider charting a transformation in your essay. It doesn't have to be earth-shattering. It can be about how you decided on your major or how your year abroad challenged your preconceptions of the world.

DOES IT SHOW YOU CAN EMBRACE FAILURE?

O YES O NO

There is a misconception in society that failure is bad and must be avoided at all costs. In truth, no great accomplishment comes without the risk of spectacular failure and/or multiple previous failures. So yes, a person can lead a sheltered existence completely devoid of the prospect of failure, but isn't that ultimately a more insidious and pervasive failure? (Answer: Yes.) The most successful people in the world are the ones who had the resilience to pick themselves back up and try again after each failure. Ask yourself, do you embrace failure or do you avoid situations where you could fail? If you embrace failure but have never failed, totally okay. But if you're an avoider, you might have issues with being too passive or not taking initiative, in which case, there's a good chance your essay is of poor quality. So congratulations! Your first failure! Once you've put yourself in some situations which required difficult decisions and you taking tangible action, you can sit down and write something much better. This book will be here waiting.

Question Forty-Two

DOES IT GO TO THE LIMIT?

O YES O NO

The word limit, that is. If the prompt says 2-pages double spaced and your essay barely makes it to 1 page or even 1.75 pages, it's a problem. That first draft shouldn't be two pages, it should be 2.5 to 4 pages. Then, in future drafts, you sculpt it down to just under the word limit, leaving only the good stuff. If you weren't given a word limit, I find 1000 words to be a good word count to aim for. Of course, don't stretch something out just to get to 1000 either. Use your discretion.

IS IT EASY TO READ?

O YES O NO

Certain essays I evaluate are a chore to get through, especially ones that come from science and engineering applicants. These essays tend to start reasonably enough, but then, they seemingly reject English in favor of jargon and robot code or something. Yes, sometimes you need to include technical elements in your essay, but try to buffer those with human speech so you don't induce headaches in your less science and math-inclined readers. Don't assume familiarity. Write it at a level a non-genius fifteen-year-old would understand. One technique that helps to make those details less esoteric is to include the real world/practical applications of whatever the heck it is that you're talking about. You didn't just build a robot, you built a robot that vacuums/flies/raps/etc. Another technique is to include your thought process regarding specific things. For example, if you want to list off some of the classes you took in college, that's going to be pretty unexciting by itself. But if you said, "X class made me more interested in X topic. I explored that topic further in the following semester in Y class." Giving that bit of subjectivity reframes it as part of your personal journey. Way better than a rehashing of you transcript. Agreed?

DOES IT EVER HAVE YOU ARRIVE AT A CROSSROADS?

O YES   O NO

For my graduate school applicants, I steer them towards including a Crossroads Paragraph. My term for a penultimate paragraph that gets introspective about their previous experiences, then arrives at the conclusion that a Master's degree would be the ideal next step. Then, the final paragraph gets into specifics about the program in question, future plans, etc. I'm not saying you non-grad applicants out there have to follow this formula to a tee, but in your essay, try to include a moment of reflection, internal conflict, a dilemma or a crisis of confidence. We've all been there, so it will humanize you.

DOES IT OFFER A GLIMPSE INTO YOUR FUTURE?

O YES O NO

Different types of essays will have different amounts of future content. For example, a personal statement for undergrad is not going to be all that focused on career goals. A statement of purpose for grad school, however, might <u>only</u> be about that. In any case, it's all subject to change. You're an applicant, not Nostradamus. Still, if you have a clear-eyed view of yourself and a clear-eyed vision of what's next (admission into an academic program), at least give us some sense that you've thought about your life in a larger context. Sometimes, this is as elaborate as a massive research proposal. Sometimes, this is as simple as, "That summer, I learned the importance of teamwork, and I will continue to be a team player going forward."

Question Forty-Six

IS IT FUNNY?

O YES O NO

If there's one thing admissions officers appreciate, it's essays with humor. I spoke to such a person last week, and he specifically brought that up. Like it or not, a good sense of humor suggests good social skills and intelligence, and yes, colleges like that sort of thing. If you really don't consider yourself funny, you can replace it with any of the following: *witty, clever, silly, whimsical, goofy, droll, eccentric, off-beat, quirky, charming, wacky.* Or you can come up with your own. But it has to be one of your defining characteristics, a word your friends and family would be used to describe you. For this question, let's not get too serious with *honest, passionate* or *hardworking*. I'm looking for something more light and

fun here. And it can't be negative. No words like *hostile,*
abrasive, profane, condescending. And be careful with
borderline words like *self-deprecating, sarcastic, ambivalent*
and *cool.*

DOES IT PASS THE SCRAMBLE TEST?

O YES O NO

If you shuffled the scenes around in almost any movie, the result would be a bewildering viewing experience. Similarly, if you shuffled the sequence of paragraphs in a quality essay, it should be just as bewildering. On the other hand, if each paragraph is so disjointed from the next that a shuffle wouldn't be that big of a deal—kind of like hitting the shuffle button on iTunes—you have a serious problem. Each paragraph should lay the foundation for the next, allowing each section to built the essay up higher. Reordering should be catastrophic, that's what passing the Scramble Test is all about.

DOES IT KEEP ITS SENTENCES RELATIVELY SHORT?

O YES O NO

I like variety in sentence lengths. A short, snippy sentence after a couple longer ones can be quite impactful. What I don't like, however, are sentences that think they can run on forever as long as there's a comma or a semicolon every few words. Stringing together combos when you're playing a fighting video game is always a good idea. Stringing together clauses in an attempt to set a Guinness world record for the longest sentence ever is never a good idea. You will be better served with writing that reflects how you speak, and most people speak in easy to digest phrase nuggets.

DOES IT MAKE THE UNIVERSITY IN QUESTION SOUND LIKE THE MISSING PUZZLE PIECE?

O YES O NO

Ultimately, that's what this entire exercise is about, right? After finishing your essay, the reader should be rooting for you to jump over that next hurdle, which is invariably acceptance to your dream school. And if the rooter happens to be an employee of the dream school, all the better! I like the analogy of the <u>missing puzzle piece</u>. Imagine your life as a jigsaw puzzle. When you start, it's just a jumble of pieces, but as you grow, you start to assemble those pieces into a pretty picture. Over time, you've created the whole picture... except for one piece—which is this particular program. You don't actually have to discuss puzzles or pieces in your essay, just convey the sense that you're a work in progress, you're nearing completion and there's just this one... last... thing...

This demonstrates that:

1. You've taken your professional and personal development seriously, hence the nearly completed puzzle.

2. You're not currently 100% self-actualized. If you were, why would you need this degree anyway?

DOES IT PASS THE CARE TEST?

O YES   O NO

There are essays that do everything else right—have an effective thesis statement, offer a unique perspective, are structurally sound—but after I read them, I still feel that there's something missing. In fact, there is. <u>Care</u>. As in, I don't have any for it. So that's your challenge, essay writer, getting your readers to <u>care</u>. This is not easy to do. In fact, I might as well rename Question Fifty "The Widowmaker." The way to make readers care is to make the essay ultimately not about you. HUH?! What about all that YOU, YOU, YOU talk from earlier?!, I imagine you saying. Yes, that's true. on the surface, your essay must absolutely be about you. But just as it's irritating to hear someone blather on about themselves without a larger point, you need a larger theme, moral or theme.

For this, I have devised the Care Test:

"Readers will care about my essay because

_____."

To pass the Care Test, fill in the blank <u>without</u> referencing yourself. Examples are:

- *it is a lesson in the importance of embracing diversity*

- *it is a humorous look at how leadership can take various forms*

- *it presents a surprising instance where honesty wasn't the best policy*

- *it is an inspirational story about overcoming adversity*

- *it is about an absurd role-reversal where boss and employee switch places*

See how any one of those is better than the following?

- *it is about how awesome I am and how I am driven to succeed. Yeah, I'm so awesome.*

What you put into your blank should fall into one of two categories:

1. *Truth, love, happiness, success, tolerance, progress, perseverance, teamwork, leadership, sacrifice, hope and faith.* I might be forgetting a couple, but if something makes you feel warm and fuzzy, if you could see a version of it on an inspirational poster, it's going to be in Category #1. Sure, these can seem hokey, but the reality is that they are timeless, universal concepts that inspire people, that make them <u>care</u>.

2. *Irony and subversiveness.* One of my examples above was about how honesty wasn't the best policy. This runs counter to what nearly anyone has ever said about honesty, so it inspires instant curiosity. News outlets do

this all the time with headlines like, "He's a Billionaire, <u>and</u> He's Homeless." The more controversial it gets, the more intrigue it will earn, but then there's more potential backlash. For college essay purposes, be careful with this. While it's easy to have a pro-faith agenda (which would fit into Category #1), an anti-faith agenda is probably not going to work in your favor. Category #2 entries will generally involve irony, like the role-reversal example above. It if sounds sort of like an interesting movie concept, it probably has the requisite curiosity factor to be considered Category #2. And when it comes to readers, curiosity is a form of... what was that word again? Oh yeah. <u>Care</u>.

DID YOU GET HELP (FROM STATEMENT GURU)?

O YES O NO

Okay, let me not be self-serving for one minute and say, you really should have some people read your essay and give their feedback. But be wary of having people really close to you—like family members or your best friend—offer their opinions. The people closest to you have a knack for throwing objectivity out the window. Instead, give it to trusted advisors and experienced writers. You know, the kind of people that have <u>others</u> approach them with things to read and offer feedback on all the time. If you really want an advantage though, you should go to the guy who wrote the book on admissions essays. Well, <u>a</u> book, at least. Anyway, my site is statementguru.com, and my email address is nived@statementguru.com. Whether or not you get in touch, I wish you the best of you luck with your essay and your future endeavors!

MOMENT OF RECKONING

How many yeses did you tally?

46-50: Your essay is an instant classic that will be studied for generations.

40-45: Impressive work. Your essay is conceptually and structurally sound, and it allows the reader to get to know you on a deeper level. From here, it shouldn't be too hard to focus on those handful of nos and take things to legendary status.

34-39: An above-average effort. You probably have an understanding of the elements that go into an effective essay, but you're struggling to combine everything into one truly satisfying whole. I hope working through this book has helped you diagnose some problems so you know what to target going forward.

25-33: My guess is you are either a good writer saddled with a bad/non-existent concept or you have a workable concept but struggle to articulate yourself on the page. In either case, you have an average essay in front of you. Sure, some applicants settle for that, but not you! I suggest you put the essay down and think long and hard about why you're writing it and what you're trying to say through it. Once you and your concept are on rock solid ground, outline and write a new draft, borrowing content from the old draft when you can.

18-24: There are issues here. Maybe you wrote this draft in a drunken frenzy. Maybe you really struggle with English. Maybe you fundamentally don't want to pursue this degree. Try not to get discouraged though, you completed one draft, which means you have it in you to complete another. But in order to make the next one work, try to draw upon the lessons from this book. Internalize them and use them to elevate your words. I have a feeling that rather than feel stifled by all these rules, you'll feel liberated that you have a path to follow, and you'll no longer have to stumble around in the dark.

17 and below: Something has gone terribly wrong. Toss your current draft and never speak of it again. You have some serious soul-searching and brainstorming to do. To make this process significantly easier, contact me at nived@statementguru.com, and I'll give you information about my Start-to-Finish essay tutoring package.

63268898R00071

Made in the USA
Lexington, KY
01 May 2017

3 1143 00928 8334